Solitary Christian Spirituality in the Modern World

Christian Thorn

Published by Christian Thorn, 2024.

While every precaution has been taken in the preparation of this book, the publisher assumes no responsibility for errors or omissions, or for damages resulting from the use of the information contained herein.

SOLITARY CHRISTIAN SPIRITUALITY IN THE MODERN WORLD

First edition. January 25, 2024.

Copyright © 2024 Christian Thorn.

ISBN: 979-8223083665

Written by Christian Thorn.

Also by Christian Thorn

Christian Spirituality: What Happens When You Follow Jesus?
Spiritual Warfare: Effective Ways to Overcome Temptations
Soul Journey: Finding Christ in Atheism
Christian Meditation Mystical Practices
The Magical Setup of a Christian Mystic
Christian Meditation Techniques for Beginners
No Worries: Let Go and Let God
Solitary Christian Spirituality in the Modern World

Table of Contents

Introduction 1

The First Step is Humility 4

Meditation 7

Read the Bible 10

Walking the Path 12

Secular Logic vs. The Divine Way 14

Two Ways of Reading the Bible 18

Imaginative Prayer 21

Sin 24

Jesus Prayer 26

Beware of the Modern World 28

Divine Providence 30

Self-Annihilation 33

Redefine the Meaning of Wealth 35

Overconsumption 38

Slow Living 41

Focus on Christ 44

The Importance of Solitude 47

Be Happy 49

A Note from the Author 51

For May

Introduction

Solitary Christian Spirituality in the Modern World is a spirituality manual that teaches how you can immerse yourself in pure spirituality and live the divine teachings while you are exposed to the complications and illusions of the modern world. These days, many people are searching for true spirituality. There is craving in the soul for something profound and deep. Although the modern world is doing its best to make man forget about the soul and what really matters in life, there are times when we feel an emptiness within us. It is an emptiness that no material thing can fill and satisfy.

A saint once said that no matter how much material possessions we gain, we will never be completely happy. The reason for this is that we are made in the image and likeness of God. We are a divine soul, and the only way to satisfy this yearning is to give to the soul what it wants. Just as fire continuously reaches up to the sun, so does the soul reaches to its Divine Creator because the only way to satisfy the soul is to unite it with God.

Solitary Christian Spirituality in the Modern World gives the foundation that you need to immerse yourself in a life of pure spirituality. Although the approach is mainly Christian spirituality, it should be noted that the knowledge and practices as revealed herein can be used by anyone, regardless of tradition and religious affiliations. After all, God is for all; Christ is for all.

CHRISTIAN THORN

Who is a solitary Christian? A solitary Christian is anyone who is yearning for true spirituality and would like to pursue the spiritual path through their own efforts — in solitary. Technically speaking, you are not completely alone because you can have the whole Kingdom of Heaven by your side every step of the way. There is simply no way that one can escape from the power and love of God. Whether you are a Christian or not, regardless of the denomination that you belong to, you can get to know God by yourself. You do not need a group or any religion to reach you the way to the Divine. Solitary Christian spirituality is a personal and mystical approach to the Divine. It involves a direct and personal experience of God. It is also worth remembering the words of the Divine Master, Jesus Christ, "The kingdom of God is within you." (Luke 17:21)

Solitary Christian Spirituality in the Modern World reveals the blueprint that you can follow to start living a truly spiritual life. We will deal with the hard facts of life, so that you will know precisely what to do. If you want to experience a life that is divine, a life that has mystery and profound meaning, then this is the book for you.

The First Step is Humility

He who dares to step toward the Divine must do so in the spirit of humility. To be humble is to be nothing. It is when we empty ourselves that we can finally be filled with divine graces. Many times, we are so full of ourselves and the things of the world that our hands could not reach up to God. It is worth remembering the words of Christ: *Whoever exalts himself will be humbled, and whoever humbles himself will be exalted.* (Matthew 23:12)

But how does one express humility? When you start your journey on solitary Christian spirituality, you need to have an open mind. Forget about what you think you already know about God. Forget about what religions and other people have told you about Christ. Instead, be an empty cup, and start with a clean slate.

When it comes to learning humility, the practice of meditation is strongly recommended. Meditation allows us to empty ourselves. It also frees the mind from so many worries, thoughts, and ideas. In the modern world, we are often bombarded with so many things and thoughts that we do not have time to be still and appreciate our existence, even our connection with God. This is why we should meditate, so that we can make time for solitude and immerse ourselves with the divine experience.

We will discuss the practice of meditation in the next chapter. For now, simply focus on understanding the importance of being humble. A wise man once said that being humble is not about thinking less of ourselves, but it is about thinking about ourselves less. We ought to realize that we are children of God. As such, we have the capacity to love completely and truly. However, many times, we spend much of our energy on ourselves, and this restricts us from the many things that we could actually do.

In our modern world, we are programmed to be somebody. People always want to climb up and look down on others. This is the way of the world, but it is not the way of God. With this kind of set up, there is no wonder why so many people today are sad, depressed, and unhappy. We have created a very adverse and stressful environment. People make themselves so important that they have no more time, not even the time for prayer. I know some people like this. They do not even have time for their loved ones. They have made themselves so important that they are always busy, trapped in a world that they have entered.

To be humble also means keeping an open mind. It is difficult, if not impossible, to understand the teachings of Christ when you do so with a mind that has been polluted by the world. The way of Christ is far above the way of the world. Hence, be humble for it is in humility that you will find stillness — and in that stillness, you will hear the voice of God calling your name, again and again.

Humility is important. Christ even said that one cannot enter into the Kingdom of Heaven unless he/she becomes a little child. Many times, the world turns us into something that seems to make us appear so big and powerful. But all these are mere illusions. We still need God, always. Let us be humble, so that we can have space in our hearts and minds to receive the graces of the Almighty.

Meditation

Let us now talk about a very important practice, and that is the practice of meditation. Many monks and spiritual seekers would say that meditation alone is enough to experience the Divine and have a mystical encounter. Meditation is also a powerful form of prayer. Not only that, but meditation will also free you from the many illusions and tricks of the world. It also stills the mind, allowing you to find inner silence and peace. It is in this silence where you can finally hear the voice of God. Interestingly, even conventional science affirms the many benefits of meditation that cover all levels of existence: physical, mental, emotional, and spiritual.

Still, it should be emphasized that meditation is, first and foremost, a spiritual practice. These days, many people get introduced to the practice of meditation as a way to release stress and relax the mind. Indeed, these are a part of the natural effects of meditation, but real meditation goes beyond the physical and it means more than a way to destress. Real meditation is an inner prayer where the soul comes in union with the Divine Spirit.

There are various meditation techniques in the Christian tradition. The meditation technique that you are about to learn is a universal technique that is practiced even by Buddhists. After all, spirituality is one, and it is for all. This meditation uses the breath as the point of focus in meditation. Breath is life. It belongs to all that has life. It is a gift from God that, unfortunately, oftentimes is taken for granted. This meditation is very easy to do, and yet it is also very powerful. It usually creates a profound peace and calmness of mind. Having said that, let us now discuss the steps:

Assume any comfortable position that you want. Close your eyes and just relax. Breathe through your nose. It is said that God breathed into man's nostrils the breath of life. This breath is life. It comes and goes, but it never ceases. A sudden break in this continuous cycle of breath would mean death. Breathe in and out. Focus gently on your breath. Breathe and let go of everything else.

Nothing should exist in the mind but the breath. If thoughts appear in the mind while you meditate, just ignore them. Only focus gently on the breath. It is worth noting that meditation should be done in the spirit of peace and serenity. No force is required. The more relaxed and in harmony you are with the natural flow of life, the more that you will reach a deep state of mind and being.

Continue the meditation for as long as you want. To end the meditation, you should gently return to your body. The way to do this properly is by thinking about your physical body. By doing so, you will be pulled back into the body. Be aware of your body, and then slowly move your fingers and toes. Once you are completely back in the body, slowly open your eyes.

The aforesaid meditation will allow you to empty yourself and have a clear mind. This is the optimum mindset to engage in spiritual things. Many times, it is the logical mind that prevents you from having a mystical experience and the unfolding of miracles.

When you meditate, you should let go of everything, even of yourself. The more that you let go, the more that your soul is going to be free to immerse in the divine experience.

Read the Bible

The number one blueprint that we can use to immerse ourselves in spiritual life is the Bible. Take note that we do not worship the Bible, but the Bible contains the divine teachings that we should follow. Now, many people feel discouraged to read the Bible because it is too thick. The good news is that you do not really need to read the whole Bible. It should be noted that the Bible is a collection of books. For starters, you just need to know the right books to read without becoming overwhelmed.

It is good to start by reading the book of Matthew. The book of Matthew also happens to be the first book of the New Testament. Simply by reading this book, you will learn about the life, miracles, and divine teachings of Christ. It is also not a long book. You will probably be able to finish reading it in just around three hours. I managed to finish it in just one sitting. The stories in this book are also very interesting, so you will really have a good time. I suggest that you schedule a special alone time, prepare your favorite tea, coffee, or any drink or snack that you love, and start reading. Be sure to use your imagination when you read. Imagine the scenes as clearly as you can, and do not rush. Immerse yourself in the reading experience. It is just like reading a good novel, except that this one is for real, which makes it even more exciting.

SOLITARY CHRISTIAN SPIRITUALITY IN THE MODERN WORLD

After reading the book of *Matthew*, you can follow up by reading the other gospels: *Mark*, *Luke*, and *John*. These are also the first four books of the New Testament. All of these books talk about the life and teachings of Jesus Christ. Pay attention to the stories, especially the teachings of the Divine Master.

By the time that you finish reading the book of *Matthew*, especially if you also read the other books, you will be equipped with the teachings that you should observe in order to follow Jesus Christ. This is the way of true spirituality, and this is the way that you ought to live.

Walking the Path

The path is Christ. Jesus said, "I am the way, the truth, and the life." (John 14:6) But what does this really mean? If Jesus is the way, how exactly do we follow Him? It should be clarified that following Jesus means following His words, His teachings. This is why it is very important to read the Bible, especially the gospels, so that we can know about the teachings of Christ.

Knowing the teachings alone is not enough. After all, even the demons are well aware of all these teachings. There are two important elements: knowing and doing. It is hard to follow unless you know; and once you know the teachings, you have to actually do them. This is how we live; and it is through actual practice and experience that we grow spiritually.

If you are not a believer in Jesus, then that is okay. In this case, simply follow the teachings. After all, teachings are ideas, and ideas are for all people without any restrictions. Just give this path a chance and see what happens. Do not worry, you can always turn around and walk away at any time that you want if ever you change your mind. Still, it is worth giving it a try. There is definitely nothing to lose, but there is so much that you can gain.

Following the words of Christ is easy when things are going well to your advantage; however, things can be tricky when you are faced or even stuck in a difficult situation. In situations like this, it is all the more important to follow the teachings. Be patient and keep on pressing forward. This is also usually an opportunity for you to witness and experience the unfolding of miracles. Many divine interventions happen when there is no other way to resolve and overcome a certain challenge. You just have to be strong and patient enough to see it through.

When it comes to following the teachings of Christ, you may wonder: Is it actually reasonable to do so? And this leads us to our next important discussion.

Secular Logic vs. The Divine Way

The modern world boasts so much about the capacity and power of humans. Many of us rely solely on human reason or logic. Although the human mind may be able to solve some problems, it is still very limited. There are many things that we still do not know. There are also things that are far beyond our understanding. It is also worth remembering that it was when Socrates said, "I know that I do not know," that he was declared to be the wisest man in the world. He became humble, and so he was exalted — giving much truth to the words of Christ that it is when you humble yourself that you will be exalted.

Secular logic or simply logic is one that depends so much on human reason. Indeed, there are many things that humans, through the use of sound reasoning, can explain. However, it must be realized that even after all these years, there are still so many things that we do not know — and many of such things are even beyond mere human understanding. This is understandable considering that the human mind has its limitations.

It should be realized as early as possible that the teachings of Christ are oftentimes different from the way of the world. Many people try to explain the divine teachings through sound and even shrewd reasoning, but this is actually a wrong approach. The truth of the matter is that there is no relation between human or worldly logic and the teachings of Christ. Many times, Christ's teachings are even the direct opposite of what worldly logic would suggest to us.

For example, the way of the world often encourages us to strike our enemies down and to be happy when our enemies have misfortune. At first, this appears to be a very common response, especially to an enemy. However, the way of Christ is so much higher than the way of this world. Instead of rejoicing for the misfortune of our enemies, Christ tells us to love our enemies (Matthew 5:44). When Jesus was on the cross, he even prayed for the people who were persecuting Him. He said, "Father, forgive them, for they do not know what they are doing." (Luke 23:34).

Many times, people like to show off their good works to be praised by men. This has also become common on social media. Sometimes we cannot tell anymore if the person is really kind or simply doing good so that they could get recognition and praise online. However, Christ teaches us to not let the left hand know what the right hand is doing. This means that you should give and do good in secret; and God, Who sees in secret, will reward you openly. (Matthew 6:3-4)

The truth is that the way of Christ contradicts the way of the world. This world that relies so much on human logic or reason has nothing to do with the way of God. Christ says in John 8:23, "You are from beneath; I am from above." It is also written in Isaiah 55:8-9, "'For my thoughts are not your thoughts, neither are your ways my way,' declares the Lord. 'As the heavens are higher than the earth, so are my ways higher than your ways and my thoughts than your thoughts.'"

If you want to have a divine experience, you must break free from the boundaries of human reason. There are times when the divine teachings will appear very unreasonable to the human mind. You just have to trust and let go. For many years now, perhaps you have been following the world of human reason, and yet you know that it is not absolute and perfect. The good news is that there is another way, and it is a divine way. However, for you to be able to follow this higher path, you must let go of the very limited and imperfect human reason. It is time to drop secular logic, and it is time to embrace a divine and oftentimes mysterious path. Do not worry, if you ever feel like changing your mind, you can always turn around and walk away — but at least give it a chance and see how it works for you.

The way of Christ can at times be difficult and unreasonable. Do not worry because things will soon become clear to you in time. There are times when we just really cannot see the road ahead. It is like driving a car in a very dark mountain, and you are just depending on the headlights as you travel. Nevertheless, gradually, you will reach your destination. The good news is that even though your vision is very limited, you can be sure that God knows all things, including every part of that mountain that you are on. You just need to trust in Him. Have faith and let go —

because if you do this, wonders and miracles shall unfold right before you. Just give it a try and see for yourself.

17

Two Ways of Reading the Bible

There are two ways of reading the Bible: the Antiochian method and the Alexandrian method. The Antiochian method is the most common way of reading the Bible. It is reading the Bible in its literal sense, as if you were reading a magazine or a novel. You take the words simply as they are. There is nothing wrong with this approach. In fact, this is also how most people read the scriptures. If you are not yet familiar with a particular story in the Bible, this is also the recommended method to read it.

Once you are done with the Antiochian method, and if you would like to gain more from your readings, you may want to use the Alexandrian method. This is also the reading approach as used by many mystics as it allows you to have a deeper and more personal experience of the sacred scriptures (the Bible).

When you use the Alexandrian method, you do not take the words simply as they are written. Instead, you view the words as a metaphor. For example, in the famous story where the shepherd David defeats the powerful and huge warrior, Goliath. You can imagine yourself as David and Goliath as your biggest problem/s in life. Know that with God's help, you can win and overcome anything.

As you can see, this method is not restrictive. In fact, it is very open where every story in the Bible becomes a living world that you can freely immerse yourself in. By doing so, every reading of the Bible becomes a form of meditation, and every story becomes a profound personal experience.

So, the next time that you read the Bible and you want to go beyond the written words, do not hesitate to use your imagination and reflect on the stories and teachings. Draw from them many meanings and apply them in your life.

The way that I prefer to do it is to read a passage first using the Antiochian method. Once I become acquainted and familiar with it, I then apply the Alexandrian method. Be sure to live the lessons that you gain by applying the teachings and your realizations in your everyday life.

The Alexandrian method and Antiochian method are the two main ways of reading the Bible. However, there is actually another way. This method is similar to the Alexandrian method but takes it a step further, and this leads us to our next subject: Imaginative prayer.

Imaginative Prayer

Imaginative prayer is praying with the imagination. This kind of prayer was made popular by Saint Ignatius of Loyola. This is a very powerful form of prayer, and it becomes even more effective the more that you practice it. It is worth noting that God is the God of everything, and that includes being the God of the mind and the imagination.

Using the imagination in prayer is a very powerful way to pray. Many mystics and monks use this form of prayer. The key here is to let go and immerse yourself completely in the imaginary scene that is taking place. Having said that, let us now discuss the actual steps:

Choose a specific scene or story in the Bible. Read it several times to make yourself very familiar with it. Next, imagine the scene. You may close your eyes when you do this to help you focus better and be more immersed in what you are imagining.

Imagine yourself as one of the characters in the story. You can also see yourself as a passerby or just an observant who happens to be in the same place where the scene is taking place. When you imagine the scene, do it in such a way that you immerse yourself in it. Do not just visualize it, but you should also feel yourself actually present in the story. How does it feel to be there? What are you wearing? How do you look? Is it hot or cold in the area? What does it smell like over there? Use as many senses as possible to fully immerse yourself in the story.

Let the story play out naturally, but do not try to control it. If it happens that the story takes a different turn or direction other than how you have read it, just allow it to do so. Just let go. The more that you let go and not try to control anything, the more powerful the experience is also going to be.

You can either be a mere passive observer or an active participant in the story. If you choose to be a passive observer, just watch and observe. If you want to be an active participant, feel free to engage in conversation and do things while you are there. For example, you can talk to the people that you see. You can even talk to the disciples and even to Jesus Himself.

See and feel the story as if it were happening for the very first time. Your knowledge of the scene will help to make the story flow without force or effort on your part. Do not judge or analyze what happens. The time to make such a reflection is after the prayer, but never during the actual experience itself. The very moment of imaginative prayer is a moment of experience and being. Forget about your physical body, even your life and worry about the physical world. Only immerse yourself as much as you can in the prayer, so that you can have an intimate and powerful divine experience. If you surrender your whole mind to the Divine, He will show you great mysteries and wonders.

Sin

Sin appears to be a big deal in the Christian tradition. Sadly, because of this, many people feel discouraged to explore the true meaning of Christian spirituality. Indeed, sin is a serious matter, but the Christian faith goes far beyond the world of sin.

A very good story to read on this matter is the story of the woman caught in adultery, which is found in John 8:1-11. Did you see what Jesus did? She defended the woman. Not only that, but she also did not condemn her. He did not even make any mention of her sin. Instead, He saved her from being stoned to death, and He told her, "Neither do I condemn you. Go and sin no more." It was that easy and free. A saint once said that our goal is not only to avoid sin, but that we must rise spiritually.

It is up to you if you want to live a life that is centered around the fear of sin or the love of God. Personally, I prefer a life that is free from all fear of sin. In the aforementioned story of the woman caught in adultery, I understood the message of Christ as if telling me to go and enjoy life, but just do not sin. Simply not sinning is not what life is all about; otherwise, we can all just sleep through life. But, if we do, it is not living. Christ wants us to cross the seas and walk over the water. He wants us to have a grand adventure with Him.

Therefore, do not allow sin or your fear of sin to limit and restrict your life. Do not sin; and at the same time, do something wonderful. After all, if you give yourself to Christ, then sin has no power over you.

Jesus Prayer

The *Jesus Prayer* is a very famous prayer, especially in the Orthodox church. However, it should be noted that this prayer is not exclusive to Orthodoxy, but it rightly belongs to all people, regardless of religion. The *Jesus Prayer* is a powerful fork of meditation, and many have reported mystical experiences through regular practice of this meditative prayer.

The *Jesus Prayer* has two versions. The short version is this: *Lord Jesus Christ, Son of God, have mercy on me.* You can also simply say, *Your Jesus Christ, have mercy on me.* The longer version, which is just a slightly longer version, is this: *Lord Jesus Christ, Son of God, have mercy on me, a sinner.* You are free to choose whichever version that you want. They are all the same. The important thing here is how often you do this meditative prayer. It is strongly recommended that you make time to do this meditation at least once daily. Having said that, let us now discuss the steps:

Assume a comfortable position and relax. Close your eyes, and free your mind from the worries of the world. Forget about all of your problems, and just be still. Next, begin to say the *Jesus Prayer*. Say it lovingly, gently, and repeatedly. As you say the prayer, gently focus on it. Focus on the prayer in exclusion of all other thoughts and things. Nothing should exist in the mind but the prayer. Let the prayer guide and lead you wherever your soul needs to be. Simply let go and let God.

Continue the meditation for as long as you want. You can conclude the meditation session by gently returning to your body. To do this, simply think about your physical body. Once you can sense your body again, slowly move your fingers and toes, and then very gently open your eyes.

Take note that just like any other meditation practice, this meditative prayer should be done with gentleness and in the spirit of peace. Do not use force. Just relax in the prayer and let go.

Beware of the Modern World

You must be very careful with how you deal with the world. This world has so many illusions and traps. It is very deceiving. There is so much evil all around us. But, do not lose hope because just as there is evil, there is also the force of good—and no darkness can ever overcome this light.

The world will continue to do its best and try to corrupt you. It will also make you so busy that you will not have time for the truly important things in life. Many people fall into this trap so be very careful. It is a good practice to reexamine how you live your life every now and then.

This world is very manipulative. Many times, people fall into the trap of the golden calf. If you have read the story of Moses when he returned from the mountain, he saw the people worshiping a golden calf. Although it happened centuries ago, it is still relevant today because many people have made money the center of their lives. It is the same sin as worshiping the golden calf in the Old Testament.

Again, be very careful because this world is highly deceiving. This is also why we need to make it a habit to read the scriptures (the Bible) every now and then, so that we can remind ourselves continually of what is really important in our lives. It is very easy to be misdirected and get lost in this world. Worse, many people in our world today do not even realize that they are already very lost and being manipulated by the evil system.

But, do not fear nor worry because if you have Christ in your heart, then you are always safe and protected because you are in the hands of the Almighty God.

Divine Providence

The teaching on Divine Providence is very important to understand. By realizing this teaching, you will be able to overcome all fear and worries. It is interesting to note that the message not to fear or be afraid is repeated more than 100 times in the Bible. There are even those who say that it is repeated 365 times, as if God is telling you not to fear every single day.

So, what is Divine Providence? It means that everything is under the providence of God. This means that everything that happens is in accordance with the will of God or at least with His divine consent. Now, this is difficult to understand, and it usually takes spiritual maturity before one can truly realize what it is all about. Rest assured that God is very much aware of everything that you are going through and everything that is happening in your life. In fact, He knows you far more than you know yourself. He knows all about your past, present, and even your future. Everything and everyone is in the hands of God. Nothing can escape His reach and control. Even people who do not believe in God are still within the power and providence of God.

When people encounter this teaching on Divine Providence, they cannot help but wonder if God is also the author of evil in this world. The answer to this is in the negative. God is not evil, although He can also create evil when He wants. But, most of the evil in the world is caused by man and other mischievous spirits. As much as possible, God wants all of us to have a good and peaceful life.

You may start to ask: If there is Divine Providence, does that mean that God allows evil? The answer is *yes*. After all, we have free will. Still, every evil thing that happens in the world happens with the full knowledge and consent of God. He is always in control. In many instances in the Bible, we can see how God turns evil into something good. This is the power of the Almighty.

The teaching on Divine Providence is something that can be realized only when you make progress in your spiritual life. Still, even if you are a complete beginner, it is good that you are aware of it. You can always rest in the assurance that God knows exactly what you are going though, and that He is always in control.

32

Self-Annihilation

Self-annihilation is not usually something that you will experience in the beginning of spiritual life. Although the term seems to be quite scary or even of a negative quality, it is actually very important and highly beneficial for you. It is worth noting that in the scripture, Christ says, "If anyone wants to come after me, they must deny themselves, take up their cross, and follow me." (Matthew 16:24)

The said denial or renunciation of the self is important because it is the catalyst for true and significant spiritual progress. Technically speaking, it is the alter ego or the false self that is annihilated. It is the annihilation of the false self, so that your real self can finally surface and become manifest—and it is the self that is divine because it is one with God.

This stage of spiritual life can be very difficult. It is like being in your own Garden of Gethsemane where there may be fear and doubts. This may also appear like some kind of depression, but its source is primarily spiritual. If you ever reach this stage, stay strong and hold strong to your faith.

There are only two ways from here: either you overcome it by going through it or you remain stuck in that terrible state for so long. The good news is that if you manage to overcome this challenge, you will soon be blessed with divine realizations and graces. Do not lose heart. God will never forsake you nor abandon you. This is just necessary for your spiritual growth. If Christ will do all the lifting, then you will not grow spiritually. Indeed, this part consists of a severe and rigid spiritual training, but it all works for your good, so that you can grow beautiful for you are wonderfully made. So, stay strong, and hold on to your faith—and Christ shall lift you up and lead you to life everlasting.

Redefine the Meaning of Wealth

What does it mean to be wealthy? In our world today, wealth is often measured in terms of money. However, we need to take a step back and see if this is really the true meaning of wealth. Let us remember that back in the old days, all the people did not have any money problems simply because money was not even in existence, and yet there were also people who were wealthy. So, what is real wealth?

From a spiritual perspective, wealth is not about money. It is wrong to measure wealth by the money that you have. Because of that kind of thinking, many people these days see and treat a person based only on how much money they make. I know some "rich" people who only want to talk with people who also have the same money as they do, and it is as if the rest who do not have that much money are not humans. Let us not forget that when Jesus walked the earth, He was not financially wealthy. Not only that, but He spent much of His time with the poor and needy. As followers of Christ, we must also not turn a blind eye on the poor. If we can, we should also help them. Let us remember the words of Christ that whatever we do to the least of our brethren, we also do it to Him; and that what we do not do to the least of our brethren we also fail to do to Him.

Instead of measuring wealth in terms of money, it seems more appropriate to measure it in terms of how much love we give. It is also worth noting the words of Saint Teresa of Avila that whoever has God lacks nothing. Regardless of your current financial position, do not think of yourself as poor. Instead, know that you have everything because you always have Christ with you. In fact, you have the whole of heaven on your side.

This does not mean that we should not think of money at all. Unfortunately, considering the setup of the world today, as long as you are exposed to the world, money is important. Nevertheless, money is not everything. It is, after all, only an object. Just like any other object, you can use it, not the other way around. Sadly, many people these days are controlled by money.

As a follower of Christ, we should stop for a moment and reconsider our view on money. We should have a healthy relationship with money. Where does it stand in your life? How much of your happiness do you depend on money?

It is worth noting that it is already a proven fact that we do not really need money to be happy. There are people today who have very little money, and some literally do not have any money at all and yet they are happy. A good example of this are the authentic and genuine monks and solitary spiritual practitioners. I have met some of them in person.

The people who depend their happiness on money always realize after earning the money that they wanted that it is still not enough. The reason for this is that there is a space in the heart that money simply cannot fill in. It may seem like money is the solution, but it is not. Most of the time, once a person earns the money, their desires even increase and continue to add up. It is worth remembering the words of Saint Teresa of Avila: *Whoever has God lacks nothing. God alone suffices.*

Overconsumption

Our world has been programmed in such a way that people keep on consuming things. Many people are caught in the trend of overconsumption. We are in a consumerist society, so consuming things has become the normal flow of things. This is the disease of consumerism. However, your life does not always have to be this way. Christ and His disciples lived a wonderful life without consuming so many things.

Consumerism is the idea that in order to be happy, we need to consume things. This also sets the programming of the world where we keep spending money on things, thinking that it will bring us happiness. This can be dangerous because it gradually manipulates the mind into believing that money is the key to true happiness. Once you get influenced by this view, your life will definitely change, even your priorities will become very mundane and materialistic.

Based on studies, it is true that we get a rush of dopamine and feel happy when we buy things, but then the happiness that we feel tends to go away also very quickly. The solution that many people come up with is to buy again and again. It is that brief feeling of happiness and satisfaction that they are chasing. However, this approach simply does not work. You will only end up chasing things without end. We must realize that the things that we are chasing after are not the key to the happiness and contentment that we truly desire.

It is not wrong to buy things, but we need to be in control of ourselves and our desires; otherwise, we will be controlled by them. We cannot be truly satisfied if we keep on looking for things outside of ourselves. It is also noteworthy that these things are all artificial and man-made. The mystics have discovered another approach—and perhaps a much better approach—and that is to seek happiness within. Let us remember the words of

CHRISTIAN THORN

Jesus: *The kingdom of God is within you.* Therefore, stop looking for true happiness outside. You will only find illusions, one after another. Instead, go within. In another ancient writing, it is said, *Search within. If that which you seek you do not find within you, you will never find it without.*

Slow Living

Slow living has been receiving a good following. Many people are now noticing that there is something very wrong with the current way of life. What is slow living? Slow living is a way of life where you live intentionally and more purposefully. Sadly, these days, so many people are just going through life just existing, without actually living. Slow living teaches us to be present in the moment—in the great moment of now.

It is also interesting to note that Jesus also lived a slow lifestyle. We can see from the gospels that He had a very huge mission that He had to accomplish in a short time, and yet He was never in a hurry. There were also many instances when He was bothered by people who needed to be healed, and He helped all of them without being in a rush.

So, how do we start living slowly? It should be noted that slow living is not about literally moving very slowly like a turtle, but it is more about the state of mind and how we deal with the things of everyday life. When it comes to slow living, there are three main pieces of advice that I have learned from my own experiences.

Number one: Do things one at a time only. In our modern world, many people are straining themselves by doing multiple things at once. Although this may seem amusing, it is not good for you in the long run. Slow living teaches us to do things one at a time only, so that you can fully concentrate and dedicate yourself to whatever it is that you are doing. Even in the life of Christ, we can see that He did things one at a time only. Although He did so many things and wonders, He did them one by one. In the same way, you can avoid the mental clutter by doing and focusing on things one at a time only.

Number two: Perhaps the most important advice that I have learned on slow living is to dedicate more time than necessary for the things that you have to do. For example, let us say that you usually spend thirty minutes to prepare for work, make it an hour. If you regularly spend about 15 minutes enjoying your tea/coffee, make it thirty or even 40 minutes. By doing so, you will not be in a hurry, and the more that you can relax and be present in the moment.

Number three: Prepare a schedule. It really helps to prepare a schedule for the things that you have to do. This way, you can keep your time organized. You can write your schedule in a notebook or even just on your phone. The important thing is to organize your time, and be sure to give everything that you have to do more than enough time than necessary. This way, you will never be in a hurry. It is also worth noting that you should do your best to avoid filling your hands with so many things, especially if it is more than what you can effectively and comfortably manage.

We are living in a society that always encourages and compels people to be productive. Although productivity is good, too much of it can also be bad, especially in the long run. It is worth noting that even God took a rest when He created the world. Allowing ourselves to become too absorbed in mundane things also takes away the time that we need for prayer. Be sure to keep a healthy balance between the work that you do for money and your spiritual life.

Slow living is for everyone, and it is also rich in Christian values as it will allow you to be more aware of the present and make more time for all the things that you have to do, including the need to pray.

Focus on Christ

The spiritual journey has its challenges. These challenges are also important because they will help your soul to grow beautifully. Just as metal has to go through the fire and take the blows from the hammer to forge the finest blade, so shall your soul undergo trials to make it strong and beautiful. In every case, do not be afraid because you can rest in the certainty that God is always with you.

The key is to keep your focus on Christ no matter what happens. It is like meditation, but it is happening in real life during the course of your daily life. It is good to read and learn from the story where Jesus tells Peter to come to Him while He was standing on the water of the sea. This can be found in Matthew 14:22-33.

Peter drowned when he focused on the waves and the strong winds. Indeed, it was reasonable to be afraid considering the circumstances. However, because of his fear and lack of faith, he started to drown. Still, know that even when you fail, know that Christ is always there to pull you up.

SOLITARY CHRISTIAN SPIRITUALITY IN THE MODERN WORLD

In life, there are also many scary waves and strong winds that we have to face. No matter what happens, always keep your mind on Jesus. It is just like meditation, except that you ought to do this as you go about with your day in real life. Regular practice of meditation will also help you to be able to do this. This definitely takes practice, but it is a very important skill to learn. In this world, there will be many problems. Although the modern world wants you to think that you are in control, the truth is that you are never in control. There are just so many things that can happen, and there are many things that you just cannot control. It is only God, in His Divine Providence, that has control over all things, even over your life.

Once you learn to keep your mind on Christ regardless of what happens in the world, you will achieve a state of mind and being that is very peaceful and serene. It is a state of being that the world cannot disturb. It has a peace that cannot be bothered.

This is the peace that transcends all understanding, and it is the peace that can only come from God.

46

The Importance of Solitude

Solitude is very important in spiritual life. We live in a world that has so many noises. It is very easy to be distracted and get misdirected. A time for solitude allows us to take a step back and calibrate ourselves back to where we ought to be. It also ensures that we are still ourselves, and that we are not manipulated by the world.

It is very easy to get too busy in this world, so busy that we no longer have time to pray and make reflections on our life. From now on, it is important that you make a conscious effort to spend time in solitude. It is a time for prayer, reflection, and meditation.

There are people who think that spending time in solitude is about going out somewhere quite far or in nature and spending time alone. Indeed, this is also solitude; however, you do not always have to go anywhere. Solitude can also be enjoyed in the comfort of your home. As such, a time for solitude does not require you to spend any money. All that is necessary is that you make time for it.

Make it a habit to spend time in solitude every now and then. It is worth noting that Christ also went to the mountains and the wilderness to spend time in prayer and solitude. It is a time alone with God. It is recommended to spend time in solitude daily. Even half an hour to an hour of solitude daily would be very helpful rather than nothing at all. However, if you are very busy, you may spend less time in solitude, but always do it because it is really important.

Whenever you can, it is also good to set a special day when you will spend it in solitude. It is like a date with Christ. Sometimes, when I am too busy, I try to make time for solitude in the evening just before going to bed. Give yourself some time and patience to adjust until it becomes a habit. The more time that you spend in solitude, the more that your relationship with Jesus will grow, and your spiritual life will flourish.

Be Happy

When you take the path of Christian spirituality, you can always be happy. You know by now that you are always in the Divine Providence of God, and that you are never alone. When you follow Christ, you do not only develop a relationship with Him. From the very moment that you follow Christ, the whole angelic realm and heavenly kingdom are on your side, including all the angels and saints in Paradise.

Even if you face serious problems and troubles in this world, there is no reason for you to worry and be afraid. Keep your mind on Christ, and He will surely sustain you. This is the adventure of our faith, and He is true and just. You can rest in the assurance that He will never leave you nor forsake you because He loves you.

This is why those who have real faith in Christ are able to remain relaxed and happy even during stressful times. As a follower of Christ, you can also do the same. Indeed, those who follow Christ always experience changes in themselves. In the sacred scriptures, it is written that those who follow Christ become a new creation. (2 Corinthians 5:17)

God wants you to be happy. In this world, we will always have problems and challenges. Christ even said that we are going to face tribulations, but that we can always find peace in Him (John 16:33). Nevertheless, regardless of what happens in this world, we can always be happy because God is with us. Because of Christ, we know that we are saved, we are free, and we are dearly loved.

A Note from the Author

The Christian tradition has a very rich spirituality, and you can experience it personally and see for yourself. Although the modern world has many traps and illusions, you always have a choice. You always have a choice if you are going to follow Jesus Christ or not. Nevertheless, it is worth giving it a shot and seeing what happens. After all, you can always turn around and walk away if you ever change your mind.

These days, I know many people from various backgrounds who are turning to Christ for a genuine spirituality. Among all the gods out there, Jesus is the One True God, and He is the One Who loves you.

Years ago, I was not into Christian spirituality. I was into various traditions and spiritual practices. I thought I was doing well, but then there came a time when I got into depression and I felt empty. In that deep and silent darkness, I found Christ. I came to know Him more and more. I also did (and still do) the teachings that are in this book. Today, I am very happy being a follower of Jesus Christ. I hope that you find the same joy and peace on your journey, and even more.

The only way to truly understand the beauty of Christian spirituality is through actual and personal immersion. You have to put the teachings into daily practice. As you do this, the more that you will draw near to God, and He will also draw near to you. (James 4:8)

CHRISTIAN THORN

Now that you have a good foundation on Christian spirituality, it is time for you to get into the adventure by taking a leap of faith. God is with you, always—all ways.

Don't miss out!

Visit the website below and you can sign up to receive emails whenever Christian Thorn publishes a new book. There's no charge and no obligation.

https://books2read.com/r/B-A-BUAZ-CIHUC

Also by Christian Thorn

Christian Spirituality: What Happens When You Follow Jesus?
Spiritual Warfare: Effective Ways to Overcome Temptations
Soul Journey: Finding Christ in Atheism
Christian Meditation Mystical Practices
The Magical Setup of a Christian Mystic
Christian Meditation Techniques for Beginners
No Worries: Let Go and Let God
Solitary Christian Spirituality in the Modern World